INFINITY

FIGURING OUT FOREVER

SARAH C. CAMPBELL

Photographs by Sarah C. Campbell and Richard P. Campbell

ASTRA YOUNG READERS

AN IMPRINT OF ASTRA BOOKS FOR YOUNG READERS

New York

Thinking about infinity is fascinating. Send your brain in search of something that never ends. See what comes to mind.

Have you ever found yourself between two mirrors, and noticed reflections of yourself that keep getting smaller, and smaller, and smaller?

While reflections between two mirrors might seem as if they could get smaller forever, this photograph shows 11 ever-smaller images. That's definitely not infinity.

So, what is infinity? Trying to define infinity—like with a photograph—is difficult. Infinity is endlessness. It is not a simple thing that exists in a single moment. It is an idea.

Luckily, human brains are more powerful and flexible than cameras. People can consider ideas that go beyond what we can see. We know this highway stops eventually but seeing a photograph that shows it getting smaller and smaller as it gets close to the horizon helps us to imagine endlessness.

Though defining infinity is difficult, there is one thing that people do every day that leads straight toward infinity. Everyone counts. The numbers we use to count—starting with 1, 2, 3, 4, 5, 6, 7, and so on—are endless.

Some people count stairs when they walk up and down. Can you count the stairs in this sculpture or are they infinite?

Infinity is mind-boggling, but thinking about infinity is useful—especially in math. In addition to being important for understanding numbers, infinity also helps define a simple geometric shape: the line.

A line is a long thin mark that never ends. The never-ending, or infinite, nature of a line is impossible to capture in a photograph. The arrow at each end of the

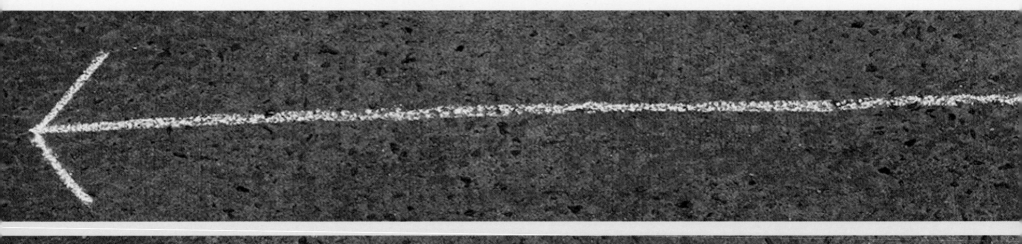

line tells our brains to imagine the line extending further, indefinitely.

A number line shows how numbers get larger and larger, passing mark after mark along the line. While any number line we could create would have an end, we use an arrow (→) and the infinity symbol (∞) to suggest the endlessness of numbers.

How high have you tried to count? To 100? To 1,000?
What were you counting? Leaves on a tree?

Birds in the sky?

What is the largest number you can think of?
No matter what large number you name, there
is always a larger number.

What's larger than one billion? One billion one (1,000,000,001). Try writing out a googol, which is a 1 followed by one hundred zeroes. It's a large number— but now add one! You see? You can always count further.

10,000,000,000,000,000,000,000,000,000,000,000,000,000,000,000,000,000,000,000,000,000,000,000,000,000,000,000,000,000,000,000,000

Did you know that the maximum number of stars a person can see from the Earth without a telescope is about five thousand (5,000)? Using data from many powerful telescopes, astronomers estimate that our galaxy, the Milky Way, has one trillion (1,000,000,000,000) stars. Stars in the sky are not infinite, but the set of counting numbers is.

Are we getting closer to infinity? The quest continues.

Thinking about infinity is tricky. You have already thought of a large number and added one, but that might lead you to make the mistake of thinking infinity is something really, really big. Remember, though, infinity is not something big. Infinity is endlessness.

To see infinity in a different way, consider what happens when a simple math problem is repeated endlessly. For example, what if we had an orange slice and took away half and repeated that, infinitely? After step one, we would have ½ an orange slice.

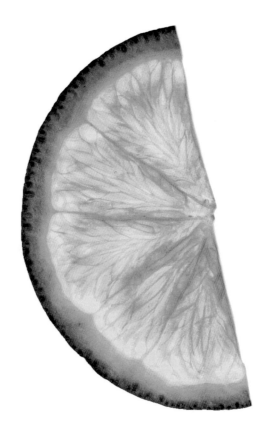

After step two, we would have ¼ of an orange slice. Step three, $\frac{1}{8}$. Can you see the pattern? Eventually, no orange is left to cut, but the math problem could go on infinitely.

Step four, $\frac{1}{8} \div 2 = \frac{1}{16}$.

Step five, $\frac{1}{16} \div 2 = \frac{1}{32}$.

Step six, $\frac{1}{32} \div 2 = \frac{1}{64}$.

Step seven, $\frac{1}{128}$.

Step eight, $\frac{1}{256}$.

We could never reach zero (0) because no matter how small the number, half that number is smaller, but not zero. Infinity is endless.

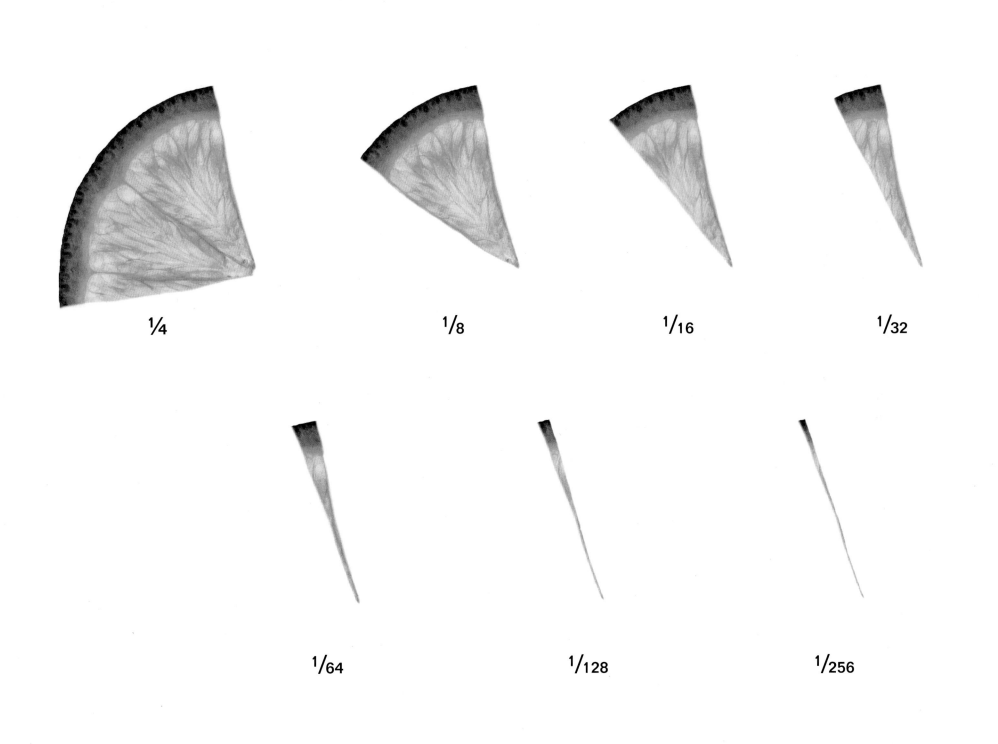

¼   ⅛   1/16   1/32

1/64   1/128   1/256

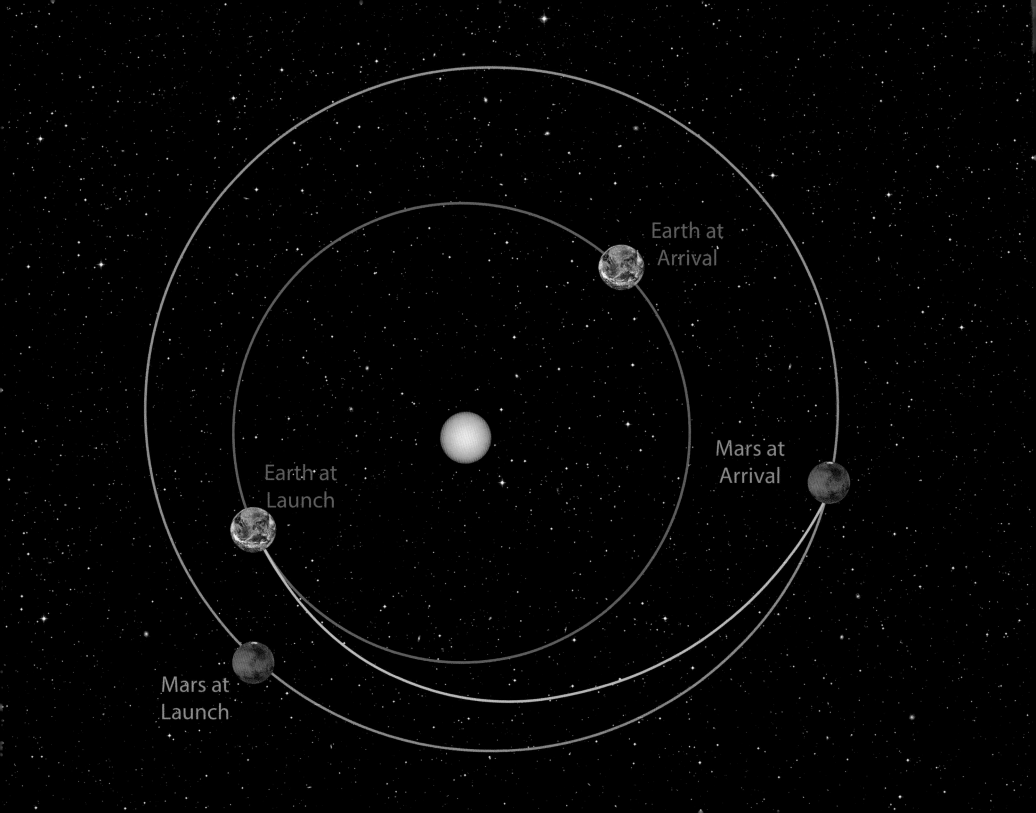

Using infinity this way—repeating a problem endlessly, and therefore creating an inexhaustible supply of small bits of precise information—is a powerful tool for mathematicians and engineers. By manipulating the bits of information, they can solve complex, real-world problems.

The branch of mathematics that puts infinity to practical use is called calculus. Typically taught in high school and college, calculus is particularly useful in solving problems where people need to predict when and where moving objects with changing weights and speeds will be located at a future time.

NASA scientists used calculus when they sent a 1.17 million-pound spacecraft carrying the Perseverance rover from one moving planet, Earth, to another, Mars, more than 292 million miles away. A triumph for infinity!

Thinking about infinity is not simple. The possibilities that frequently come to mind—like mirror images or distant horizons or counting stars—are not really examples of infinity. No quick snapshot from the mind's eye can capture it entirely. Instead, we must expand our brains to hold seemingly contradictory ideas. Infinity isn't a number, but it figures into problems containing the tiniest fractions and the most humongous numbers. It shows itself in the endless march of time and in the continuing birth of new stars in our ever-expanding universe.

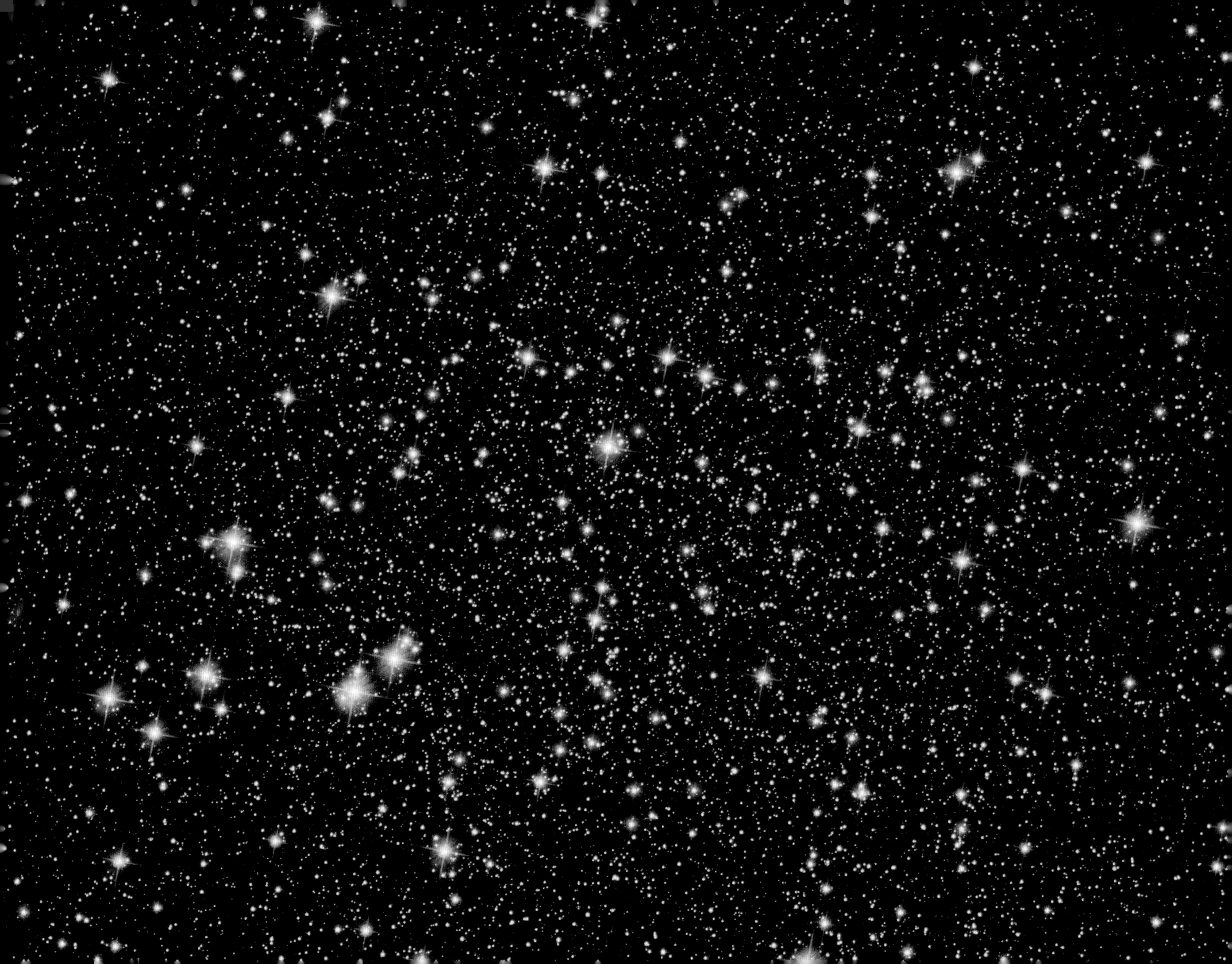

The next time you find yourself counting stars in the sky, remember that even though the number of stars is finite, your mind has no limits.

You can always imagine one more.

Author's Note

When I began my research for this book, I discovered that though infinity was a known concept to scholars in ancient Greece and India, it was considered mysterious and, even, suspicious. Something endless that could not be seen by human eyes or captured in a number or shape did not seem to fit into the ordered realm of mathematics. If useful at all, they thought infinity belonged to philosophers and religious scholars who contemplated and wrote about ideas beyond human experience.

These prejudices about infinity lasted for centuries. Then, in the 1870s and 1880s a German mathematician named Georg Cantor, published groundbreaking work that established a place for infinity in the heart of mathematics. Specifically, Cantor proved that a set could have infinitely many members. The most common example of an infinite set is the set of numbers we use to count: (1, 2, 3, 4, 5, 6, 7, 8, 9, 10, 11, . . .). Other infinite sets include even numbers, odd numbers, and prime numbers.

Cantor also demonstrated that some infinite sets are bigger than others, and that we can develop precise mathematical tools for measuring these different-size infinities. Like many visionaries with radical new ideas, Cantor was attacked by establishment scholars of his day. Over time, however, other mathematicians verified his work, and built upon it, establishing one of modern math's key pillars: set theory.

Just as mathematics has developed over centuries, people have also invented stronger tools for observing and exploring the Earth and outer space. Some of the images in this book were captured by photographers for the National Aeronautics and Space Administration (NASA) and the U.S. National Park Service (NPS). While it remains just as impossible to photograph infinity as it was for the ancients to come up with a simple definition of it, I have used photographs throughout this book to reveal glimpses of its power and beauty.

The Infinite School and the Surprising Results of Adding with Infinity

Adding two numbers usually results in a new, larger number. Let's say you have 10 rings, one for each finger on both hands. And then someone gives you another ring. You would have 10 + 1, which equals 11. If you put one ring on each finger of both hands, you would have one extra. So, 11 is more than 10. But, adding a number to infinity, which is represented by the ∞ symbol, does not result in a new number. Endlessness plus 1 is still endlessness. So, ∞ + 1 = ∞.

To see how this works imagine an infinite school. This infinite school—with its bright, never-ending hallways—contains infinite classrooms, infinite teachers, and infinite students. It also happens to be completely full. Every classroom has a teacher and students. One day, a school bus arrives carrying a new teacher and the students in her class. The teacher asks the principal for a classroom. At first, this request worries the principal at the infinite school because she knows her school is completely full, but then, remembering something about infinity, she comes up with a clever solution.

The principal instructs all teachers to move their students to the classroom with the next higher number. So, the teacher in Room No. 1 moves students to Room No. 2, the teacher in Room No. 2 moves students to Room No. 3. The teacher in Room No. 3 moves students to Room No. 4, and so on. This leaves Room No. 1 open for the new teacher and students. Once she moves her things in and starts teaching her students, the school still has infinite classrooms, infinite teachers, and infinite students. And it is still completely full.

Now, you may be thinking, as I was, *why didn't the principal tell the newly arrived teacher to take her students to the end of the hallway to the last classroom?* The reason is that infinity has no end. So, that means the infinite school has no last classroom at the end of the hall.

Now, imagine what would happen if 20 school buses arrived with 20 new teachers and classes. The principal could instruct the teacher in Room No. 1 to move to Room No. 21 and the teacher in Room No. 2 to Room No. 22 and the teachers in Room No. 3 to Room No. 23. Do you see the pattern? After all the moving, the 20 new teachers could occupy the rooms numbered 1 to 20. And the school would still be completely full.

Now, imagine what would happen if infinite school buses arrived carrying teachers and students. This would seem to give the principal big worries. Actually, though, the principal has a ready solution. The principal could instruct all teachers to move to the room with a number twice as big as the number of the room they are in. So, the teacher in Room No. 1 could move students to Room No. 2. The teacher in Room No. 2 could move students to Room No. 4. The teacher in Room No. 3 could move students to Room No. 6. The teacher in Room No. 4 could move students to Room No. 8. Do you see the pattern? After all the moving, every even numbered room (2, 4, 6, 8, 10, . . .) would have a teacher and students in it and every odd numbered room (1, 3, 5, 7, 9, . . .) would be empty. Then, the principal could welcome the infinite teachers and students into the infinite school. And it would be completely full.

Symbol Glossary

∞ —the symbol for infinity

$\rightarrow$ —an arrow symbol, indicating a rightward direction

$\leftarrow$ —an arrow symbol, indicating a leftward direction

Word Glossary

astronomer—a person who studies matter and objects in the sky, such as planets and stars

calculus—the branch of mathematics concerned with rates of change and the finding of lengths, areas, and volumes

engineer—a designer and builder of machines, processes, structures, or systems

finite—having certain limits

fraction—a number such as ½ or ¾ that represents a part of a whole

galaxy—one of the very large groups of stars and other matter that are found throughout the universe

geometric shape—a form with specific properties related to points, angles, surfaces, and solids. Examples include lines, circles, squares, and rectangles.

googol—name for the number 1 followed by 100 zeroes

horizon—the line where the land or sea seems to meet the sky

infinite—having no limits of any kind

line—a long, thin mark that never ends

mathematician—an expert in mathematics, which is the science that is concerned with numbers and their properties, relations, and operations and with shapes and their structure and measurement

maximum—the highest quantity or value

NASA—The National Aeronautics and Space Administration (NASA) is the United States government agency responsible for science and technology related to air and space.

number—mathematical quantities we use for counting and measuring

number line—a line without ends whose points are matched to numbers by their distance from a given point labeled zero

pattern—a set of characteristics that are displayed in a repeating way, though, not always as exact copies

planet—a heavenly body other than a comet, asteroid, or satellite that travels in orbit around a star

set—a collection of numbers or objects that have certain properties that distinguish them from other numbers or objects that don't have those properties

telescope—an instrument, often tube-shaped, for viewing distant objects by focusing light rays with mirrors or lenses

universe—all matter and energy, including the Earth, the galaxies, and all outer space, regarded as a whole

Further Reading

nasa.gov/stem

nps.gov/kids

Ekeland, Ivar. *The Cat in Numberland*. Illustrated by John O'Brien. Chicago: Cricket Books, 2006.

Hosford, Kate. *Infinity and Me*. Illustrated by Gabi Swiatkowska. Minneapolis: Carolrhoda Books, 2012.

Schwartz, Richard Evan. *Life on the Infinite Farm*. Providence, Rhode Island: American Mathematical Society, 2018.

Acknowledgments

For suggesting that I write about infinity, I thank Sarah Lyu. For help with the mathematics of infinity, I thank Michael Frame and Daniel Waxman. For reading many drafts during the eight years it took to write this book, I thank my parents, Patty and Dave Crosby; my sister, Jessica Crosby-Pitchamootoo; my aunts, Peg Dillon, Kathy Welde, and Mary Leonard; my friend, Julie Owen; and my friends and critique partners in the Louisiana and Mississippi chapter of the Society of Children's Book Writers and Illustrators. For editorial help, I thank Andy Boyles, Andrea Cascardi, Rebecca Davis, Barbara Grzeslo, Julianna Lauletta, Brittany Ryan, and Liz Van Doren. For providing subjects and spaces for photography, I thank Simms and Jasper Powell (and their parents, Joy Parikh and Greg Powell), Emilie Hebert, and Two Dog Farms. For sharing her likeness for the mirror image, I thank Jocelyn DeZutter (and her mom, Stacy). For going the extra mile to provide a lovely photograph of a high-powered telescope, I thank Christian Obermeier. For helping me get feedback from young readers, I thank Anelyse George, Bruce Golden, Linda Williams Jackson, Jenny and Blake Jarvis, Ashley Rogers, and Rhoda Yoder. I thank Richard for everything.

Picture Credits

Unless otherwise indicated here, photographs were taken by
  Sarah C. Campbell and Richard P. Campbell.
365 Focus Photography/Shutterstock: 9.
Albert Beukhof/Shutterstock: 14–15.
Neal Herbert/National Park Service: 28–29.
National Aeronautics and Space Administration: 24, 27.
National Aeronautics and Space Administration/Jet Propulsion
  Laboratory/United States Geological Survey: 24.
National Aeronautics and Space Administration/Goddard Space
  Flight Center/Solar Dynamics Observatory: 24.
National Aeronautics and Space Administration/European Space
  Agency/G. Piotto (Università degli Studi di Padova)/A. Sarajedini
  (Florida Atlantic University)/Gladys Kober (Catholic University of
  America): 27.
Christian Obermeier: 18–19.
United Launch Alliance: 25.
Wikimedia Commons: 30.

For Graeme, Nathan, and Douglas

Astra Young Readers
An imprint of Astra Books for Young Readers, a division of Astra Publishing House
astrapublishinghouse.com
Printed in China

ISBN: 978-1-62979-875-2 (hc)
ISBN: 978-1-63592-826-6 (eBook)
Library of Congress Control Number: 2021918554

First edition

10 9 8 7 6 5 4 3 2 1

Design by Barbara Grzeslo
The text is set in Folio Std.